Just the Ticket

A Comedy

Peter Quilter

Samuel French — London
www.samuelfrench-london.co.uk

CHARACTERS

Susan, an eccentric, untidy and endlessly chatty woman, ideally aged 60 years old (or she could be 50 years old) The character can be played by one woman, or shared between several women. (See author's note)

SETTING

Flexible set within which furniture and other items will simply and quickly establish location. The show probably works best played without an interval. The running time is approximately 90 minutes. If an interval is preferred, it should be placed at the end of Scene 3

SYNOPSIS OF SCENES

Just the Ticket had its world premiere at the Ensemble Theatre in Sydney, Australia in February, 2011. The production was directed by Sandra Bates and starred Amanda Muggleton

AUTHOR'S NOTES — IMPORTANT

Just the Ticket features only one character – Susan – and she may be played by just one actress, taking the play on as a comedy monologue. However, Susan can also be played by three different actresses. Or four actresses. Or six actresses. Each playing the role of Susan in different sections of the show. In order to make this work, and allow the cast size to be flexible, the play has been divided into twelve sections.

If you were to present the play with three actresses, each actress would perform four of the sections. If you did it with four actresses, they would perform three sections each. If you did it with six actresses, they would do two sections each. Where the change of actor happens in the middle of a scene, the next actor would come on to continue the scene wearing the *exact same costume.*

The actresses – however many of them there are – should endeavour to make the character of Susan similar. Similar, but not identical, because the interpretations of different actors is part of the fun. But the audience should nonetheless feel that they are watching the same character, only with a slightly different spin on it. Much like we accept different actors playing James Bond. The character is essentially the same, but each actor brings their own personality to the part.

You can share out the twelve sections as you wish. Though the neatest choice would be to present actors throughout the play in the same order. ie. Section one for actor one, Section two for actor two, Section three for actor three, etc. and then repeating the actors in the same order for the rest of the play. But equally you could mix and match as the mood takes you!

Note that after the twelve sections, there is one extra part at the end of the show, *Final Section,* which will bring all the actresses on stage together. Though, of course, if the play is to be performed by just one actress as a monologue – then ignore all of the above!

Whether for a team of one, three, four, or six – I hope you have a lot of fun with it.

PETER QUILTER

COPYRIGHT MUSIC

The author would like to dedicate this play to:

Gary, Claire and Joseph Quilter

Section 1

Music plays — Frank Sinatra singing "Come Fly With Me"

An airport lounge. A row of plastic seats. A coffee vending machine in the corner. Enter a bare-footed Susan, having just survived airport security. She walks on stage carrying a large plastic tray in which she has her jacket, bag, jewellery, purse, watch and tickets and passport. In each hand she carries a shoe. And hanging from either side of her mouth is her belt. Susan is a rather awkward woman, either 50 or 60 years old — depending on the actress playing the role — with poor taste in clothes and a worse haircut. She wears little makeup and makes no effort to look attractive. Though full of life, she appears at first to be one of life's victims. Sad and messy, or amusingly eccentric, depending on your viewpoint. She stumbles, flustered, to a seating area, almost losing her balance and falling flat on her face. When she avoids the tumble, she declares to nobody in particular —

Susan Nearly had me there!

She throws all the items down, removing the belt from her mouth. She turns to what we suppose is another passenger sitting nearby

I feel like I've done half the journey already. It's quite a trial, isn't it? I think it's a conspiracy. All this airport security. The whole thing is designed with the sole purpose of degrading you *and* making you spend half your life savings on a bottle of water. Still — you can't let it spoil your fun, can you? I wouldn't mind if they'd done a quick body search — but no such luck.

She laughs to herself. She puts her shoes on

And I do love a man in uniform. I had to take off everything: belt, jewellery, watch, necklace. I thought for a minute there I was being mugged! Then I had to put it all in a tray, remove my shoes, and march through when they waved me forward. I'm sure this is what they do to you when you enter prison — only the guards are friendlier.

She puts on her jewellery and watch and belt

And I thought I was doing so well. I had my Munchkin-sized toothpaste in a clear plastic bag and — well, I don't know. When did it all get so complicated? In my day, you just walked right through waving your passport in the air. You could be carrying five cans of gasoline and a set of steak knives and no one would have noticed. Still — all done now. Did you take yours off? Shoes, I mean — did you have to...? Oh, well I did. That's odd. You look far more dangerous than me.

Everything now sorted, she sits down. Then suddenly panics

Tickets!

She hunts around and quickly finds them

Here they are. It's all right — panic over... Not going very far without these... Although *with* these, I'm going very far indeed. All the way round, in fact. The world, I mean. Second time... I'm going around again — round again. Doing the whole thing again. Going around the globe — full circle. All a bit daunting. I haven't slept. Worrying and worrying. But at least I made it to the airport. So that's a start. Anyway — listen to me yapping away — you carry on reading your book. Don't let me disturb you.

Only a brief moment passes

I'm off to Australia — have you ever been? Oh — you should. I had a wonderful time — the first time. This is my second. Only I'm going on my own this time — last time I was with others, so it was less of a worry! Still, we all need an adventure now and again, don't we? Where are you off to? Milan? Well, I hear that's not so much an adventure as a punishment. But you're going with your wife, so that'll make it easier. You can share the spaghetti — like those two dogs in the Disney film. Suck one end each!

The passengers suddenly get up and leave

Oh, you're off then? OK — bye.

She turns to a passenger on the other side of her

I think I put them off. People don't like striking up conversations with strangers these days, do they? Everyone sits on the metro in big cities trying to avoid catching anybody else's eye in case they're a murderer. And if someone *does* talk to you, you know you're going to get invited to their church. In rush hour, they say you get your bum caressed. But I haven't found that to be the case. And I stayed going round on that bloody train for hours.

This other passenger leaves too

Oh, are you going as well? Everyone leaving in a hurry — is there a fire or something?

She sits quietly for a second, then looks to a passenger sitting opposite her

Just you and me then! I'm Susan, by the way. I talk a lot. What's your name? — Your name? — Oh, are you foreign? No speak the language? No? Not a word? Oh, right... no point me yapping then...

She carries on anyway

Never could keep my trap shut. I could if I wanted to, of course — but, I don't know, I just don't seem to want to. It's like voluntary Tourette's. It's the nerves, I expect. I'm a very nervous person. So I make other people nervous around me. Even my cats are stressed out. And that's why I never married! Because otherwise I'm pretty bloody irresistible aren't I!?

She laughs to herself

You don't have to answer that. And you won't — because you don't understand a word I'm saying do you? But it's all right — I'll calm myself down. I just wish I wasn't here on my own. What a stupid cow. Nobody goes on an adventure on their own, do they? You always find someone. Though I did try. But friends see me coming and they cross the road. Which is very odd. I think one look at my face and they suddenly remember they have to get their hair done — so they dash across to the salon opposite. Without another moment's thought. They should use me in evacuations. We have to clear the building immediately — send in Susan to start a conversation. — My friend Julia *nearly* came with me but she's not one for jumping on aeroplanes. She gets travel sick going down the garden. But I thought "well, what the hell" — just because I'm on my own, why should that stop me. — Not that this is some great act of rebellion, I'm not doing it just to

declare my free spirit and independence to the world. I'm not trying
to prove anything. It's not a last hurrah before old age — it's not me
versus the menopause. Been there and done that. Got the T-shirt and
the hot flushes. Though it did effect me — "the change" — and my
chances of finding a good man. Problem with being a woman is that
you do have to go through the change, and the problem with men is
they *never* change — so all in all... Where are you off to?

She points at the people and then at her ticket

Oh that's nice — a few days on the beach. It'll be three weeks for
me — just like last time. — I did it several decades ago, you see. This
trip. When I was twenty. I went around the world with some other girls
— it was amazing. And this year I'm — well — I'm not telling you
my age — but let's just say my breasts are falling faster than the stock
market.

She laughs to herself

Anyway, I thought, it's high time I re-lived that *wonderful* trip and
went round again. Around again. Re-live my youth, as it were. So here
I am — with the same dream and the same rucksack — but with forty
years of extra baggage! (*Change this to thirty years if appropriate for
the age of the actress*)

The passengers opposite now leave

Oh, are you off? Well — have a nice flight. Hope you don't crash or
anything.

SECTION 2

Susan stares out front, now talking to herself

Susan   I can't believe I just said that. I must be even more nervous
than usual. I'm blurting things out. — Lucky they didn't understand...
Don't know why I'm like this. — Well, it's obvious, *of course* I'm on
edge. I'm going around the world all on my own. Anyone would be
hysterical. No wonder I'm talking to myself...!

*She sees another traveller, in the distance, staring at her. She calls over
to her*

It's all right — just talking to myself. Helps get rid of the nerves. I'm not mad or anything. (*To herself*) Well, of course, it might be I'm completely mad — but let's just say I've not been diagnosed. I'm an unknown — an enigma in terms of my mental incapacity or otherwise... You know, I really don't have a clue what I'm saying. I really must be petrified. (*Calling back to the passenger*) So sorry. Just ignore me... Oh, you are. You've gone. Good decision. Step away from the lunatic.

She sits in silence for a moment, swinging her feet about beneath the chair. she decides to check the information on her tickets

The name's right, the date's right — boarding soon. No need to check I'm at the right gate — I've already done that twice.

She checks she's at the right gate

Shame nobody came with me. It would have been nice to be sat here solving a crossword with somebody — taking turns at guarding the bags as the other goes to the loo or buys some useless magazines.

We hear an airport announcement: "Flight one-seven-four to Paris, please board at gate twelve. Last call for flight two-two-nine to Buenos Aires — board at gate twenty-seven"

Middle-aged frump extremely bored at gate thirty-five. No, not bored. Waiting. Just waiting... I should have bought one of those MP3 players — or an iPod thingy or a laptop. I could be listening to Frank Sinatra or zapping aliens as we speak. Not that I'd ever work out how to use one of those machines. I haven't bought a thing in the last twenty years that hasn't required my nephew to come over and give a full explanation and crash course. The manuals either don't exist or have been written by someone who has no understanding of the human mind. I think every home computer should be sold with a thirteen-year-old. He comes in the box along with the cables. And he stands there and explains how to do everything. 'Cos without him you're stuffed... I suppose that's why people have children. To save phoning for an engineer. It must be a comfort to know you don't *have* to learn how to operate the DVD recorder. Your acne-ridden teenager will save you. That's their purpose on earth. To lead their parents through an ever-changing world. It used to be the other way round...

The first traveller returns and she speaks to him again

Yes, still chatting away. Now I'm even starting to bore *myself*!

She gives him a little wave goodbye as he carries on walking

Maybe I should get myself a drink or something. Something to calm me down, relax my nerves — coffee!

She hunts around in her bag for loose coins

I'm going to need some change for the machine... I love hot drinks machines. They're terribly clever. You push a few buttons and out pops a fresh cup of coffee. Still to this day, I've no idea how they work. When I was a little girl I used to think there was a man sat in there with a kettle and a jar of Nescafé. I used to think how terribly uncomfortable it must be, to be sat in that little box all day. I've never really got the image out of my head and still thank the machine when I'm finished. Unless it doesn't work, of course, then I give the poor bugger a good thump like everybody else.

Having found a handful of change, she gets up and crosses the stage to the hot drinks machine. She puts in the coins and selects her drink

As she does so, we hear another airport announcement: "We remind passengers that for security reasons, they should keep their belongings with them at all times. Any item found left on its own will be taken away by the airport police and immediately destroyed. In accordance with the government's announcement of a red danger level for possible imminent attack, passengers should report any suspicious persons or actions to a security officer. Armed law enforcement operates in this airport. Always be vigilant and aware of potential terrorism... Have a relaxed and pleasant flight."

Susan's drink emerges from the machine. She takes it and, after a moment, leans into the machine

Thank you! Have a nice day!

She stands nearby, or else wanders about the stage, sipping her coffee

Oh — my change.

She goes back to the machine to search for her change with one hand while balancing her coffee with the other

Inevitably, she spills some coffee on the floor

Oh bugger! (*Calling out*) Anybody got a cloth...? No? Oh, wait a minute —

She goes to her bag and takes a complete toilet roll from it

Oh yes — always bring a toilet roll whenever I travel any distance. Not that I usually go very far. Just don't want to get caught short. Always good to have emergency supplies. Things you might need and also a snack to eat. I meant to bring a packet of biscuits, but there was none in the cupboard — so I bought some bread rolls and a few tins of sardines.

She shows us the two tins of sardines

Thus immediately lessening my chance of a holiday romance... But who am I kidding...

She uses the toilet roll to clean up the spill

I've always been accident-prone. Just like my mother. She'd drop more food on the floor than actually ended up on the table. I think it was her own way of dieting. And of course she got worse as she got older. Though she was never a young woman — not to me. She was middle-aged by the time I emerged. She had her children very late in life. Delayed having kids as long as she could — as though it was a suspended sentence.

She returns to her bag and puts the toilet roll back inside it

In her final years, her house was chaos — and it generally ended in disaster whenever I took her out for the day, especially if we tried to eat something. An ice cream was the worst. There seemed to be a total breakdown in communication between her mouth and her right hand. The ice cream cone would rocket forward and upwards with great enthusiasm but generally bypassing her mouth and slamming elsewhere. Into her nose or ear, or God knows where. And there she'd sit. With raspberry ripple all over her cheeks and a Cadbury's Flake wedged in her bi-focals. Everyone that happened to be around us would have a giggle — while I reached for my trusty toilet roll. Oh, what joyful adventures we all have to look forward to in life.

She forms the now wet toilet roll into a ball and puts it to one side

SECTION 3

Susan   But she'll be glad that I'm travelling. Her generation never got
very far. Though she did manage to do Venice in peak summer on her
honeymoon. Returning home with tales of urine-stenched canals and
a town square so full of tourists that you couldn't see the town square
— just the tourists. And here *I* am — off to Australia! She would be
so proud... No, actually, she'd think me bonkers. What with all the
terrorism and dangers of flying. I've got it all covered, though.

She gets a newspaper article from her pocket and unfolds it

It's got it all here — in this newspaper article I found. (*Reading*) "In
the event of a fire on board the aircraft, make a low posture and head
for the exit; in the event of lack of oxygen, reach for the mask above
you; in the event of one engine failing, lean into a brace position
supported by the seat in front of you; and in the event of *both* engines
failing, move back in your seat, put your head between your legs, and
kiss your arse goodbye...! (*She laughs*) Actually I made that last bit
up. I thought about sending it into their letters page. But you have
to write it down and get a stamp and go to the post box — and it all
just seems too much trouble. Which is what I think getting older is
perhaps all about — finding everything suddenly so complicated and
requiring great effort. Which is why I'm here. To do something that
I would have done — that I did — many decades ago. And *making*
myself do it again. Despite the effort, despite the aching back and high
blood pressure and the — complete fear. To be on the edge, to feel
alive again. Before all my *agains* are just too much trouble. And life
is as dull as — coffee from a machine. (*She turns to the machine*) No
offence!

*She finishes the coffee in one gulp and then looks for a litter bin. Seeing
none, she stuffs the dirty toilet roll into the empty cup*

At what point did all the litter bins disappear? Did it happen one night
while we were all asleep? Suddenly we're walking around with empty
bags of crisps for half an hour — just waiting for the miracle of a
bin...! I'll hand it in at passport control.

She puts the cup to one side and sits down again

I do quite enjoy passport control. Like I said — a man in a uniform... It's always the same — always with a fake air of seriousness. They take a quick look at you — study your features. Then they look at the picture in your passport — and try not to laugh. I don't think they actually check the details around my photo — they just wave me through out of sympathy. My passport picture is exceptionally bad, though. And they make you live with it for ten years. It looks like one of those photos they have on those "before and after" TV programmes. You know — where they show you the "before" picture with a housewife resembling an old sack of potatoes, with no make-up and with a hair style that looks like it was put together by a two-year-old with a knife and fork. "This was Susan *before* the make-over. And now here she is afterwards — exactly the same...! Well, you can't polish a turd...!"

It's not that I don't want to look pretty — but however much effort you put into lips and fringe, it doesn't solve your body problems. Some of us just aren't the right shape. I see all these women wearing dresses where the breasts support it and then the gown just flows directly downwards, pausing only to briefly kiss their hips. But my body doesn't go straight down. It's like a slalom assault course. So many unexpected curves and bumps firing in all directions — the material doesn't know which way to turn. So you start going for baggy — which of course makes people think it's even worse underneath than they imagine. And you go for dark and plain, so the eyes don't even linger on your figure because the outfit is so dull. And then suddenly you realize in your effort to not look bad, you've given everybody a reason never to look at you at all. And so nobody does. Though I did do flashy once — my cousin's wedding.

A dark brown skirt and then a top with lots of layers and creases in shimmering gold. I looked like a Ferrero Rocher...! Though not quite good enough to eat. And before you ask — no, I've never been married. I'm completely single. Not that I'm advertizing. Oh, I don't know if I could even cope with it now. It might be nice to have the occasional wrestling match in the bedroom and someone to fix your plumbing, but — well, you get used to your own timetable... And buying your own plunger. I like an empty house, knowing you can walk in the door and do whatever you want. It'd be a bit of a shocker to see some hairy ape sat there watching a TV programme about car crashes...

I've not always lived alone, though. No, no — I lived with Julia — the friend that nearly came with me. We were just friends, of course — in case you were thinking there was something lesbian going on. No — that's not for me, thank you. Not that I've anything against it. I often think that lesbianism is not so bad an idea — especially when you consider the alternative... Julia got a boyfriend. I never expected her to actually move out and go to live with him. And I felt betrayed when she did. I couldn't afford the mortgage on my own and her departure downsized me from a suburban house to an apartment so small that the kitchen and bathroom were right up against each other. You can have a pee and toss a pancake at the same time...! But it's better than nothing. And at least I was near to Mother. Bringing her a magazine in the morning and a bit of dinner in the evening. She liked a pasty, gravy and mashed potatoes. And a tin of peaches. Pretty much the same every day. I used to sometimes bring her a bit of fish or a nice salad — but I couldn't bear to see the look of disappointment on her face. She didn't like change. She was pursuing a life without surprises. Which sounds quite good in theory. But it isn't — believe me.

We hear an airport announcement over the tannoy: "Announcing the boarding of flight QS one-seven-two to Sydney Australia."

That's me!

She starts gathering all of her things together

The announcement continues: "Now boarding at gate thirty-five."

I'm off! I'm off!

She runs across to the far corner of the stage, forgetting to take any of her things with her

She exits

A second later, she runs back on and back to her things

She collects everything together. Just as she appears ready to depart, she suddenly freezes

What am I doing? What am I doing! I can't do this on my own. I don't have anyone to share it with — I don't have a — I'm frightened of flying! This journey takes hours and hours. I can't sit still for that long. I'll end up talking to everybody! The person sat next to me will be suicidal before we've left the ground. I'll be so troublesome. And the nerves! I'll have a heart attack right there on the plane — they'll have to carry me off like a piece of luggage. I can't... I can't! — Look, by not going, I'll actually *save* money. I only lose the cost of the flight. But I'll save on the hotel and the meals. If I stick to sardines and rolls at home for a month, I could recuperate all my costs. Oh Julia, you silly old tart! Why didn't you come? You think that gorilla of a husband couldn't have coped without you for a few weeks? Though — that wasn't the real reason, was it? No. I know what it was all about. You didn't want to go back again. You couldn't bear to walk again in your twenty-year-old footsteps. Because if you did — you'd realize you wasted *all* of the years that followed. Seeing how you'd let your young self down. How you'd let me down. That's why it's painful to go back. That's why it hurts.

She drops all her bags on the floor and becomes silent

Airport announcement: "Final announcement for Flight QS one-seven-two to Sydney Australia. All passengers immediately to gate thirty-five please... And that includes you, Susan. So get off your fat arse and get on the bleedin' plane."

(*To the audience*) He never said that. I made that last bit up... Well — what's to do then? They say you can't go back. That it's never the same. That you should only ever look forward. But when I look forward, I don't see anything. It's all a blur. Like looking at the years ahead through the rain. So going back seems the only way forward. Yes — forward I go to Australia. Or — I suppose — *down* to be more precise.

Airport announcement: "Susan! Are we going to have to drag you on to this bloody plane?"

Susan suddenly leaps to her feet

No... No you're bloody not! I'm coming! I'm coming!

She charges across the stage with all her belongings

Don't leave without me!!

She exits

Snap blackout

SCENE 2

SECTION 4

Music plays: Frank Sinatra singing, "Come Fly With Me". Lights rise on the bar area of a hotel in Sydney, Australia. The bar stretches across downstage, so that Susan is facing the audience as she sits at the bar with her handbag. Lined up along the bar are four different and extravagant cocktails, plus a few empty glasses of champagne that she consumed earlier. She is a little tipsy, but not too much at first. As the rest of the scene progresses, her state of drunkenness will increase

Susan   I made it! Here I am! The other side of the world! And we didn't crash. Which was lovely. I do ache a bit, though. It was such a long flight. The sun came up and down whenever it fancied and the attendants announced it was night time even though we all knew it was actually four in the afternoon. But they broke the boredom by offering up food in a plastic tray that tasted like — a plastic tray. And we had some movies — and the rest of the time I filled with talking to everybody. Oh, you know me, I make friends very easily. I must have spoken to the chap next to me for half the flight. He was lovely. His name was James. He was a very good listener — though I think he nodded off a couple of times there. At the end of the flight, I insisted that he give me his phone number so we could continue our conversation here in Sydney. And you'll never guess what — he wrote down the wrong number! I've tried it three times — it doesn't exist. He's going to kick himself when he realizes...

Anyway, you survive the flight and then have to battle your way through security and find yourself a bus and then — *voila*! Just a little later and here you are at the bar of the very hotel you stayed in as a twenty-year-old — in Australia! Jet-lagged and half comatosed, but happy. And I've already found an old friend — Bill the barman! He was here at the bar first time round. I didn't recognise him to be honest. He was of course much younger back then. Now he has enough facial hair for birds to nest in and a belly you could stand a pint on — but that's OK. It's what's underneath that counts... Apparently. It was him that recognized *me*. He said I had the same sparkle in my eye. "Oh!" I said, "I think all my sparkles ran out years ago". "Not from where I'm standing," he said. "Oh!" I said, "You're a cheeky one" and then he said "oh" and I said "oh" and I've forgotten what happened after that...

Well, it's that long flight, you see, you suddenly slip into a coma for five minutes. Still, after a brief snore in Neverland, I came back and he remembered there was this group of girls and that one of them was a bit accident prone and embarrassed and — well... I go in shops every day where people don't recognize me from the day before. But Bill the barman recognized me. It's a long way to come to be remembered. Anyway — what was wonderful about Bill — what's *still* wonderful — is that he knows all about cocktails. And he's lined them all up for me like a fashion parade. I'd better explain myself, in case you think I'm an alcoholic.

She snorts and laughs at this and almost falls off her bar stool

These were the drinks we had — me and the girls — when we first came here in our twenties. Pauline (*pointing at her cocktail*) liked a Piña Colada — that's pineapple and coconut and rum. Julia liked a Tequila Sunrise (*pointing to it*) which has orange juice and tequila and — sunrise. And then big Debra liked a Brandy Alexander (*pointing to this*) which is brandy and cream and other bits and pieces. And then my beverage of choice was my own invention — a Super Susan. Which I created by randomly picking four bottles from the selection in front of me and getting the barman to run them all together in a blender. And it was delicious! Problem is that they've since moved all the bottles and this new concoction looks a little less super than the original. Still — Bill says that if I drink this one last, it will taste delicious regardless of what's in it. Your *fourth* cocktail always tastes good, he says. So this is my tribute to the girls — who may not be with me in person second time around, but are at least colourfully represented by good ol' Bill here on the bar. So let's give Pauline her moment in the spotlight. Get your arse over here, girl.

She pulls the Piña Colada to her and takes a long gulp of it through the straw

It's very sweet and thick. That's not gonna get through you in a hurry. Pretty umbrella. Pauline would have liked that. She would have taken the little umbrella home as a souvenir. She was a kleptomaniac of anything that was free. She gathered up the shampoo bottles and cotton buds of every hotel she ever stayed in. And she'd clear out the mini-bar too without paying anything. Replacing the whisky bottle with cold tea and putting it back. Water for the vodka and very strong black coffee to refill the coca cola. If she was any tighter, she'd squeak. But I suppose she needed to be to fund her smoking. I remember she sat here at the bar the whole of that first night, unable to sleep due to the time difference, and she just smoked and smoked until you couldn't really see her at all. Just a large cloud. She couldn't go a moment without her cigarettes. She even had a Marlboro hanging out of her mouth when she walked down the aisle. Fortunately, he was a smoker too — the guy she married. Sixty a day — so they were a good match. And they moved out to the country and bought a lovely three-bedroomed ashtray together...! Where they procreated two nicotine-stained children, and named them Benson and Hedges... No, I'm joking! I made that up! The kids were called Karen and Christopher. I went to the christening. They didn't ask me to be godmother, but I did get to help on the sandwiches.

She takes another sip of the cocktail

She probably couldn't taste this — everything tasted of tobacco, she said, even her husband... She never kept in touch — not in recent years. Well, you smoke as much as she did and that's all your leisure time gone... Actually when I say I never heard from her, that's not strictly true. There was never any effort on her part to keep in touch as friends, but you would get the very occasional phone call if there'd been some bad news. You know the sort — you don't hear from them for years, but then they give you a bell out of the blue just to let you know that someone has died.

Section 5

Susan re-enacts the call

Susan "Oh, hallo Pauline, how are you?" (*Mimicking Pauline's voice*) "Well, not so good — bad news..." "Oh dear. Has something happened to your husband?" "No — unfortunately he's fine". A pause at this point as she lights up another — she's switched to Marlboro Lights. They have half the tar in them, so you can smoke twice as many. A few puffs to kick-start the heart and then she continues; "Remember Robert Mears?" "No, I don't think I do, to be honest." This doesn't stop her — "Well, remember Alison? The bar-maid at the hotel by the river who had her nipples pierced." I said "Yes" to this in order to be polite, but I actually had no memory of a hotel or indeed a river and let alone some woman with bling on her breasts. What's the point of rings on your tits anyway? It's not like you can hang them up on a hook when you get home. Still, she carries on — "Alison was married to Barry Smith — who ran the butcher's shop by the church and his niece was Beverly — who worked in the hairdressers across from the police station — and she was married to Robert Mears."

At this point, by some miracle or desperation, I did actually remember Beverly the hairdresser and that the fact she was near the police station was fully appropriate as her sense of styling was criminal. "Oh yes!" I cried, "*That* Robert Mears, I *do* remember him... (*Now a gloomy tone*) Why? What's happened to Robert?" "Oh, nothing," she says, "But the German who lives in the house opposite fell off a cliff...!" Why should I care!? But Pauline just thought I should know. In case I wanted to buy a sympathy card. Which I did, in fact. And sent to Pauline's husband... I did go to the German's funeral, though. Well, it was a Thursday — there wasn't much else to do...

She sips some more and then calls over to Bill, the barman

Bill! I think there's too much coconut in this — I'm a tourist, not a monkey. I'm no expert, I'm not saying that, but it does seem far more nutty than is completely necessary — much like myself. Just make a note for the next customer.

Back to the audience

Bill has asked for feedback — given that I'm sampling a variety of cocktails, he thought it might be an opportunity to improve his recipes.

Back to Bill

I think I'm done with this one. But leave the glass there. It's to remind me of my friend Pauline, who can't be here.

Back to the audience

I did send her a card about my trip, but no reply. Maybe she moved house... She had a bit of a fling with some Aussie fella while she was here, as I remember. Well, we were all *very* young. We never met the gentleman in question, but they left the bedroom door open and Debra saw a little brown bum popping up and down — so we presumed the worst. I don't know why it is that some women just seem to attract men all the time. Even after their husbands die, they have a quick turnaround. I just don't see how the conveyor belt works. I mean, I have men that I talk to, but how does it move from there along to the notch on your bedpost and then the ring on your finger? I think my problem is that I don't know when men are flirting with me. I always had suspicions about George at the corner shop. Well, his name wasn't George because he was from Arabia — so it would have been something completely different. But the previous owner of the shop — a six foot tall white man with a ginger beard — was called George. When he retired, this small, dark Arab man took over the shop and everyone just carried on calling him George as though nothing had changed. But that's beside the point — George — Arab George — would always have a little chat with me whenever I came in for a packet of cakes or something. And sometimes he'd chuck an out-of-date can of tuna into my bag for free — or add a couple of extra potatoes into the basket. Now is that flirting? Offering me his King Edwards? How do you know...? Pauline would have known. She had that Aussie's trousers off before he'd had time to say "G'day". Just one flash of her yellow teeth and he was a goner.

The lights dim on stage

Hey, what's going on?

She checks her watch

Oh, — it's midnight! They'll be starting the disco. Bill forewarned me. Every night when the clock strikes twelve they convert the bar into a funky dance hall... Whether it's completely empty or not.

A glitter ball effect sends sparkles of light around the room

I used to love to dance. But not now. Not at my age. Much more dignified to just sit at the bar with my friend, Bill.

She gestures to Bill, but then realizes he has gone

Oh, — he's gone. Bill...!? Oh well... In that case — let's move on to my friend —

She pushes away the Piña Colada and replaces it with the Brandy Alexander

Debra! This was her drink back then. What's in this one? Oh yes, that's right. Brandy Alexander for Debra. Poor old Debra...

She takes a sip of it

Oh, now that's nice. Very nice, Bill. Very brandy-like. (*Looking around*) Where's he gone? (*She takes another sip*) I'm not surprised she liked this — anything that clogged your arteries was just the thing for Debra. She was a big girl — and that created a bit of a problem on the plane over because she needed two seats really. As she squeezed down the aisle, knocking the magazines from people's hands, you could see the face drop in horror of every passenger who had a vacant seat next to them. "Oh, don't let it be me..." I don't know if she was aware of it — the reactions, I mean. I was in a café with her once where the waiter called over another member of the staff for no reason at all other than to come and stare at her. But she just ordered her hot chocolate and carried on. If I noticed it — how come she didn't? Maybe she just blocked it all out. I don't get it — she wasn't even that big. I mean she was double the rest of us, but she couldn't cause a total eclipse or anything. Yet they'd gawp at her like the circus was in town... I suppose I was the bleedin' clown.

SECTION 6

Music suddenly begins, filling the room. It is Boogie Wonderland *by the band Earth Wind & Fire. Susan is at first taken aback by the sudden music, but relaxes into it as she consumes her second cocktail. After a few moments, she starts to move her shoulders to the music and this gradually develops until she is spinning on her chair, waving her arms in the air and singing along to the music. After a while, she looks around to check nobody is watching and, unable to resist any longer, she launches herself on to the dance floor, to boogie along to* Boogie Wonderland. *She dances — quite bizarrely by most standards — and with co-ordination that has been affected by excess alcohol. We watch her dance, taking in the full extent of the dance floor. Seeking to do something wild, she decides to climb on to the top of the bar. She does so — with no great ease — and then continues to boogie from up there. Brandy Alexander still in hand, she dances precariously to the music.*

After a while, she catches the attention of Bill — who has just returned from music duty — and it is clear that he has instructed her to get down from the bar. She gestures that she will obey his request and proceeds to manouevre herself off the bar and back on to ground level. This proves not to be an easy task and we witness her inelegantly scrambling downwards, bottom first.

At one point, her skirt gets caught on a hook as she descends — with the result that it lifts up as she slips down, accidentally exposing to the audience the rear view of her industrial sized underpants. She ends up in a pile on the floor, though has somehow managed not to spill a single drop of her Brandy Alexander. She takes another gulp from the glass and then staggers back to the centre of the room, where she dances joyfully to the final part of the song. It ends and she is ready for more. The song that follows, however, is something aggressively modern (gangsta rap or something else that's violently contemporary). She freezes and looks aghast — like a rabbit suddenly caught in headlights. Grimacing, she makes a few attempts to identify how she might dance to this, but soon accepts that the modern world has suddenly caught up with her.

Crouching into a low position, she crosses back to the bar as though a soldier avoiding enemy fire. Once at the bar, and fast getting a headache, she realizes how she might block out the noise and reaches into her handbag. After hunting around, she takes out a pair of ear plugs and sticks one in each ear. As she puts in the left plug, the music cuts out at stage left. As she puts in the second plug, the music cuts out completely. She smiles triumphantly

Susan I never was a good sleeper. These plugs can block out anything. Even 2014. (*Note: adjust the year accordingly*)

I don't know how you're supposed to dance to that. Though Debra would have found a way. Always the centre of attention on the dance floor, life and soul of the party. Debra was such a laugh. She loved a good joke, however dirty, and she loved her food. Didn't care about her weight at all, which was the most wonderful thing. Though on her wedding day, once she'd put the white dress on, she did say that she thought she looked like a giant meringue. Which I think was a cry for help... Now I think back on it, we should have all disagreed with her, but she said "meringue" and everyone just nodded sympathetically. The husband got a job the other side of the country and that was more or less the last we heard of her... Until Pauline phoned with bad news.

She holds the cocktail glass close to her heart

And we miss her... Funny thing is, I think Debra would have actually come with me. She'd have loved that chocolate mousse they served up as we crossed the ocean. I expect I'd have given her mine. She used to enjoy food so much more, you were happy to stay hungry in exchange for the pleasure of seeing her wolf it down. I admire people who eat for pleasure. We're all so concerned with calories and salt content that we've forgotten food is meant to taste good. I know a lot of very healthy, skinny people who enthusiastically load themselves with salad and couscous, tell everyone how young and alive they feel, and then go to bed completely miserable. I mean to say — happiness is not to be found in gluten free pasta and soya beans. Debra knew that. It wasn't the weight that got her in the end — in case you were waiting for me to say she choked to death on a beef sandwich. No — it was some awful hereditary thing that struck all of a sudden. It had been sitting there quietly in her DNA just waiting to crash the party. An unwanted gift that had got passed down through the generations. And now she's sat up there — at the great buffet in the sky.

"I'm not looking for a long life," she once said to me, "I'm looking for a good life." Quite right too. Unless, of course, like me, you're still looking for *any* kind of life... I see all the possibilities laid out before me, but I never seem to go out and grab it. I was born an eternal window shopper... But not today. Today — jet-lagged, a little drunk, with chocolate mousse down my blouse and hardly a clue what I'm doing — I'm living it. Whatever it is. Not just existing — *living*. There's a big difference. Don't sip it. Drink it.

With this, she downs the rest of the cocktail in one gulp. Then she puts the glass to one side and reaches for the next cocktail — a tequila sunrise

I think I'll take Julia out on the terrace — and better take her friend with her.

She collects her handbag and the two remaining cocktails, and with one in each hand she proceeds to walk around the full outside edge of the stage. As she does so, the bar setting transforms into a moonlit hotel garden

SCENE 3

SECTION 7

Susan sits down on a garden seat and removes her ear plugs

Susan   It's still warm here, even at night. You feel like the moon is tanning you. So many little sounds as well. I don't know if they're birds or lizards or — well, it's all very tropical. You have to check under the toilet seat before you sit down, apparently. There can be an entire zoo down there. Oh — there I go again — ruining a perfect romantic evening. And it really is beautiful. (*She looks up at the sky*) Sprinkled with stars and a light breeze. I'm sure the moon is brighter here. How lovely... A perfect moment in a perfect place. There's only one thing missing ——

She looks at the empty space beside her on the garden seat

— a packet of crisps! (*A short pause*) Oh, hang on, though.

She puts the two cocktails down and roots around in her handbag where she discovers a small bag of aeroplane snacks

Nuts from the plane! "Perfect" just got even better.

She eats a handful of the nuts and then offers some to the Tequila Sunrise

Nuts, Julia?! (*Slight pause*) Bloody Julia. She was my last hope. (*To the cocktail*) You left me on my own again... I'll never understand it. I thought we made a great team when we lived together. We had lots of sensible arrangements — such as — if one of us wanted to bring a man home for the evening, then the other would excuse herself politely and go to the café up the road for a few hours to have a piece of cake... In the first month, I put on five kilos. She did like her men — all shapes and sizes. Tall, skinny, old, young — I don't know if she was dating or doing a survey. She concluded, after her extensive research, that there were three types of men — the good-looking, the sensitive, and the vast majority. Though, of course, armed with this wisdom she ends up with a man who looks like an extra from *The Planet of the Apes*.

People will probably say I'm jealous. Not jealous from wanting a fella for myself, but jealous of these men — any one of whom might take my best friend away from me. Which is exactly what happened. I'd have forgiven her if she'd come away with me on this holiday — but it clashed with her "operation". Rumour has it that she's having her skin tightened again. It's like elastic as it is. You throw a pea at her face and it bounces half-way across the room. They pull that face any tighter and her eyes will pop out and she'll be speaking from round here. (*She gestures to the far side of her cheek*) They tuck all the excess skin behind the ears. She must have enough back there for a set of luggage by now... Julia spent her whole life trying to look younger than she actually was. The men she dated would have to wait so long for her to prepare herself in the bathroom that by the time she emerged they wouldn't have cared if she looked like Frankenstein. They were just glad to finally get some fresh air. The hair styling was all part of this military operation, each follicle sprayed, gelled and dyed to within an inch of its life and the matching jewellery carefully chosen from what all the previous boyfriends had lavished on her. She wore them like trophies.

Well, I suppose it was easier than sticking their heads on a pole. And then there would be all those fashionable outfits. Julia strictly followed the colours of the season. If the stores and magazines declared that the colours of the summer were yellow, cream and strawberry — then yellow, cream and strawberry is what she'd bloody wear, regardless of whether or not it made her look like a trifle. And there's no flexibility in this. Oh no. If blue was not mentioned, then all her blues stayed locked in that vast wardrobe. As though having personal choice and individuality was breaking some kind of law. She thought that obeying the fashion announcements of each season made her match up with all the young people out in the street. Oh, it all sounds like too much hard work to me. I think you should age gracefully if you can and disgracefully if you can't — because trying not to age at all is a battle you'll never win. Though she perhaps deserves a medal for trying... But just between you and me — she doesn't look human anymore. She's got these big fat lips which she has injected regularly to give her a very large pout. Oh they are scary. I used to let her kiss me on both cheeks, but now I'm worried she'll suck my earrings off. It's not that I mind people trying to look good — I just get confused when they try to look different. Why do you want to look like somebody else? You should live with what you've got. Make the very best of it, or — as in my case — just abandon all hope.

Oh, I don't mind being a bit of a mess. And there are advantages to being able to get yourself ready in ten minutes flat. It frees up all that extra time to sit around wondering what to do with the rest of the day... Be nice to have a couple of nice outfits for my holiday, though. Maybe I'll go shopping tomorrow. I'll send Julia a text. Ask what the colours of the season are — and then buy the opposite. I could get all dressed up. Bill might like that. Bill the barman. He's very cute, you know, in an out-of-focus kind of way. With that receding hairline and that generous belly. Well, you don't want anyone too gorgeous do you? They'll just use you and throw you away... Which sounds pretty ideal after four cocktails... Speaking of which...

She sips the Tequila Sunrise

Nice choice, Julia. Very delicate, very sophisticated. — Down in one.

She drinks the whole thing in one large gulp. This excess hits her about two seconds later and she suddenly goes queasy

Oh dear — that may not have been a wise decision... (*Calling out*) Is there a gentleman here who can help me to my room? (*Slight pause, no answer*) I'll go back to the bar. Bill will push me in the right direction.

She puts the snacks back in her bag and then very unsteadily gets up on her feet and takes a few paces away. Then she pauses

Oh wait — I'm completely forgetting myself.

She goes back to the seat and collects her final Super Susan cocktail

The Susan. An acquired taste, but not quite so bad once you get over the initial shock. Looks almost attractive in the moonlight, or any other dim lighting.

She wobbles on her feet

You know — I think Bill might have taken a bit of a fancy to me. Well — he's always giving me these cheeky winks. Though of course that might be his nervous twitch. It's so hard to tell after a few cocktails. Don't you find...?

She wanders unsteadily across the stage, taking a sip of her drink. Lights fade to black-out as music rises: Men At Work singing I Come From a Land Down Under

SCENE 4

SECTION 8

Lights rise on Susan at the beach. She wears a full-body striped swimming costume reminiscent of the 1930s and sunglasses. She is sitting under a parasol and is eating a doughnut. She removes her sunglasses and gestures towards us with her pastry. Music fades out

Susan Stop press! Big news! — Bill the barman kissed me! Also — in Los Angeles — there was a tremor of three point two on the Richter scale. I tell you this in order to answer your question, "Did the earth move?" Yes it did. Albeit on the other side of the planet. And in answer to your next question — no, I'm not joking about the kiss and no, I did not imagine it. Absolutely not. I did not imagine it!

A pause

Oh God... I hope I didn't imagine it... I haven't got the courage to ask him. So the answer may be lost forever. And this conundrum has led to the inevitable — pastries!

She takes a bite

To be fair — I'm pretty sure there was some *kind* of kiss. Very possibly nothing more than a peck on the cheek to say "goodnight". Not that that stopped me from over-reacting. I believe I swooned like I was in some nineteen-thirties romantic movie and exclaimed a breathless "Oh Bill...!" As though he had just bought me a dozen roses and suggested

I immediately live with him in his mansion in Melbourne. (*Slight pause*)Not that Barman Bill has a mansion in Melbourne — he has a caravan in Kirribilli. Parked on his brother-in-law's front lawn. But either way, the kiss was an act of politeness and my reaction to it was about as subtle as this bathing outfit. I apologized to him this morning over a poached egg. He said I shouldn't give it another moment's thought. Which is very generous of him. The manager of the hotel was equally forgiving — in terms of the dancing on the bar — and thanked me for providing the security staff with hours of entertainment. They have security cameras, you see. You have to be careful these days, you never know when you're being video recorded. People can watch you crossing the street, riding a bus, buying bananas. I had no idea my life was so compelling. They used to say when I was at Catholic school that God sees everything. Now we're giving God a run for his money.

Still, no cameras here on the beach — apart from that one that takes satellite photos of everywhere. But I've got my parasol, thus sparing the internet geeks from view of my lovely swimsuit. I found it in a charity shop, secondhand. Whenever I see anything that makes me look like a tube of toothpaste, I can't resist. They don't make them like this anymore. The woman in the charity shop said it belonged to an old spinster who used to live above. She had her breakdown in it — while holidaying in Tenerife. Which, let's face it, is likely to drive anybody crazy. It was a bit of a job squeezing into this. I really could have done with three strong boys and a large shoehorn, but we managed. And now we're stuffed right in there. Though I may never get out of it again.

She bites the doughnut

Not if I carry on like this. It's not my fault, though, because you see the doughnut came in the lunch box provided by the hotel. Doughnut, ham sandwiches and a carton of apple juice. An exotic journey through the culinary delights of Australia! You'd think they'd throw in a bit of baked kangaroo or a slice of koala — but alas, no. (*Slight pause*) Still, food's the last thing you think about when you're here baking in the sun and watching the waves mess about. It's lovely. I arrived around noon. I couldn't manage any earlier because of the hangover. I think the worst culprit was the Tequila Sunrise. A drink designed to ensure that you will never actually *see* the sun rise. You'll be in bed all the next day with a bag of frozen peas on your head. But Bill made it look so pretty. I expect I shall venture to the bar again tonight — but no more cocktails. And no more kisses. I shall accept only a little wave goodnight, or perhaps he could give me a little wink from one of those twinkling eyes of his. (*Slight pause*) I'm not smitten. Not at all... Well, it wouldn't be normal, not at my age... I should be content with all that nature has laid out here before me. Who needs a man when you've got sunshine and pastries.

She takes another bite of her doughnut and puts her sunglasses back on

The waves are much bigger than I expected — and the sea is bluer. Or is it the ocean? I was away at school the day they did Geography. Either way, the water has sharks in it — so no swimming for me, I'm staying right here. "Jaws" will not be getting a bite out of this striped delight. Not that he'd consider it. I'd probably frighten him off. What with me looking like a cross between a walrus and a zebra crossing.

She takes a further bite of the doughnut

I wouldn't be as tasty as this. Oh, I do love a good doughnut. Not great for the figure though, obviously. High in cholesterol, fats *and* sugar— which means one bite and you're risking life and limb. But that's me — I live on the edge.

She consumes the rest of the doughnut in one mouthful

Bill, I should mention, also appears to throw caution to the wind in the dinner department. He sports a belly which has reached that marvellous extent where it wobbles not only up and down but also side to side. He calls it his "happy belly". It represents his joyful rejection of a healthy lifestyle. My friend Debra's belly had much the same variety of suspension and could indeed move in four directions at once — an action which had the ability to frighten small children. But it came — always — matched with a smile on her face.

She removes her sunglasses

Oh, I miss that smile. It was a smile as sparkling as a Christmas tree. And twice as hopeful. (*Slight pause*) Aah, hope. That ridiculous emotion. Hope has a lot to answer for. Not least in December. It's the reason — against all logic — that we still put up decorations at Christmas — in the hope that for once it might live up to all the hype. I don't know — you put up lights and bells and trees and fake snow and Santas and reindeers and candles and — well it all looks like the start of a marvellous party. Which always ends up with you slapped on the sofa in a state of deep depression, watching *The Sound of Music* and farting like Armageddon. And as you gaze at the lights and bells and trees and snow and Santas and reindeers and candles, you wonder again why you went to all that trouble when Christmas is clearly never ever going to be the same as when you were six. And even then it was over-rated because everybody insisted on buying you socks. My mother thought it was practical. And my father didn't want to spoil us. Chance would be a fine thing.

She gets up and moves downstage to the water's edge, taking her carton of juice with her

Daddy never had a good word to say about any of us, let alone spoil us. My parents were so desperately concerned about any of their children becoming big-headed that they never praised us for anything at all. Least of all me. It wasn't like I had much to be big-headed about. A child that shows off is, it's true, a terrible thing. But it's preferable to a child with nothing at all to show off about...

SECTION 9

Looking out to sea, Susan catches the eye of somebody passing by in a boat. She calls out to him

Susan Oh, hallo! I saw you messing about with that boat when I was finding myself a spot to settle down. Is it seaworthy? ... Good — but no engine? ... No, well, it will give you muscles using those paddles. Also handy if a shark attacks. ... Yes, of course there are, didn't they tell you? Oh, don't look worried — they're not going to go for you — you're all skin and bone. They want something to chew on, but you'll be all crunchy. So you ignore what I said — if you see a fin above the water, don't worry... It's when they dive underneath the boat you have to worry.

The boatman suddenly departs

Oh, there he goes back to the beach! Not so much as a goodbye. He's going much faster this time.

She waves goodbye to the boatman

Maybe I said the wrong thing. Wouldn't be the first time... I expect I was a slightly annoying child. So my parents did their best, I suppose.

And I can't really blame them for Christmas now they're not even around. In fact, nobody seems to be around these days. After my first trip to Australia, Christmas was a very grand affair — all four of us girls got together and we looked at all the photos of our trip again and laughed at all the things that happened. And we did that for years until one by one they drifted off. Julia started avoiding those kind of get-togethers pretty soon after the operations. She didn't want to be confronted with images of what she *really* looked like. But Debra would always drop in on Christmas morning, to bring some silly gift. On one occasion, it was a vibrator she picked up in Thailand. I didn't really know what it was so I just put it on the mantelpiece with some holly around it. That did make Debra laugh. Oh, and when she laughed! It's still echoing even now... Especially now.

She inserts the straw into her carton of apple juice and takes a sip

We never had long-life apple juice in a plastic carton with a straw in my day... We had fruit.

She takes another sip as she looks down at her feet

I suppose I could dip a toe in.

She reaches her foot out and reacts to it touching the water

Ooh, it's quite warm. Maybe I'll go in a bit further — later in the week. Worries me to go in on my own — I'm not scared of getting wet, I mean I wouldn't go all the way in anyway — just enough to frighten the seaweed. It's just that it's one of those activities that you want to share. As the water hits you and you get surprised by the waves and you lose your balance — all those activities that make you laugh in embarassment and reach behind you to grab their hand.

She reaches behind as though to grab someone's hand. With nobody there, her face saddens

I don't mind eating alone or shopping alone — I don't mind sleeping alone. I just sometimes wish I had...

She reaches behind herself again, still nobody there. She shrugs

But you don't always get to choose what you have... I've no regrets, not really. I sometimes wonder if I'm the fortunate one. I mean I'm not addicted to cigarettes, I haven't gone before my time, and I've not had to resort to plastic surgery. Here I am, a life survivor, with good

lungs and the same face I started out with. Lucky me! I said this to
Julia only recently and she looked very surprised... Although of course
Julia *always* looks very surprised — her face can't do anything else.
It's permanently fixed in one emotion — the eyes wide open and the
tight face looking aghast. So she's aghast walking the dog and aghast
loading the dishwasher and aghast buying vegetables. God help her if
anything truly surprising happens, her face won't know which way to
turn.

She spots someone else in another boat

Oh look, there goes another... Oh it's Bill! Bill!

*She waves enthusiastically, then realises she's in her bathing costume
and rushes to cover her chest with a towel and her groin with the
lunchbox. This done, she returns to the shoreline and calls out to him*

What are you doing out there? You'll get eaten. ... Yes, eaten! Look
at you — there's enough there to keep the sharks going for a month.
You're like a floating buffet. Are you coming ashore? I can spare a
ham sandwich. ... Oh, okay — I understand. That's all right. I'll see
you at the bar later — after I've been sightseeing. Though you're quite
a sight yourself! ... Oh, he's off. Bye then! Bye Bill! Bye!

*She waves enthusiastically at him, bouncing on her feet like a little girl.
Then he makes his way into the distance*

I'm not smitten... Can't get distracted. I've got things to do. Got to go
back to all those places we went to first time around. I'll take lots of
photos. Then when I get home, I'll suddenly turn up at Julia's house
to show them to her. I can't wait to see the look of surprise on her
face...!

*Snap to black-out. We immediately begin to hear the piano music that
will continue in the background of the next scene. It plays at full volume
at first, fading into the background when the scene begins*

Scene 5

Section 10

Lights rise on Susan, now all dressed up for a black tie evening in the hotel ballroom. She is standing in the corner of the room by the entrance. We hear gentle piano music playing in the background. She wears high heels and a cocktail dress bought that day from a charity shop. Her breasts in the dress appear slightly larger than before. She holds a flute of champagne

Susan It's Saturday night, so I got all dressed up in my favourite dress. Actually it's only been my favourite dress for about four hours because I bought it this afternoon. I was very lucky that they had something in my size — as the lady behind the counter said through her clenched teeth, "Well, you do have quite an unusual shape..." So having splashed out on the dress, I thought I should get some shoes to go with it. This may have been an error as I'm not good in high heels. Which is part of the reason why I'm still standing here in the corner of the room. I'm not convinced I can make it across to the drinks table without a major accident. It's not so much wobbling on the heels and then falling over that bothers me. I'm more concerned about the debris that might be created en route. As I go down, one hand might throw the champagne glass randomly at a New Zealander while the other punches into the groin of an unsuspecting Filipino. So the issue is not what happens to me. It's like being a drunk driver. It's not so much the risk to yourself, it's that you're putting everyone around you in danger.

Don't know why I bought heels. I suppose I didn't want to disappoint Bill by arriving in a lovely evening gown, trainers and a pair of thick socks. Not that he would have minded. He's very forgiving. Anyway — the decision was made and here I am still at the launch pad awaiting clearance. Who on earth designed these things anyway? They cause everyone to ruin their posture and crawl to a clinic for treatment. I think the designer was in a conspiracy with chiropractors. The only way to avoid embarrassment is to stay right here for the evening. I've already got my champagne and I've threatened the waiter so that the vol-au-vents head at decent intervals in my direction. So better not to end up in a heap on the floor just for the sake of crossing the room. It could get the evening off to a poor start. And that would be a shame because it's a lovely event — they're celebrating the hotel's anniversary — I'm not sure how many years but the staff have been allowed to invite one guest and Bill asked me along. This was very flattering at first, although he did go on to say that he couldn't think of anybody else. He's unmarried, doesn't make friends easily and has just the one sister who, apparently, has lost her charm since she got out of prison. So here I am. I think I brush up quite nicely. And the lighting here is quite dim which, as you already know, adds to my allure. The other great advantage of being positioned in the corner, at the entrance, by the door, is that it's always easy to make an exit. If you're "mid room" and desperate to leave, you have to battle through a field of apologies and excuses in order to fight your way out. But right here at the entrance, you can slip out quietly and nobody notices. The only *negative* of being by the door is that people come in and hand you their coats and umbrellas. I feel it's impolite not to take them... One person even gave me a tip!

She shows us the money she was given

So I shall get myself a pastry later. I'm quite used to cloakroom attending anyway. As a young lady I had a summer job at one of the theatres in the city. I would attend the cloakroom or store people's bags or else tear their tickets. It was a very nice job as most of the ushers were unemployed actors or trainee singers or musicians. There was often more talent in the foyer than on the stage. You need to think about it a little when you go to a show or concert — the person pointing you to your seat might be the next Olivier or Placido Domingo. But then again, they might be the next *me*!

Slight pause

The job was nice, but the members of the public could be very difficult. Especially if the theatre was showing an opera. Then all the people, however common they were in reality, felt that they were instantly sophisticated and intelligent just by virtue of the fact that they'd bought a ticket. They *must* be a middle class and elegant couple because they're off to the opera! But only five minutes into the show, the whole veneer would fall apart, as one turned to the other and exclaimed, "Oh shit, it's all in Italian". And then you get those attending the Kirov or the Bolshoi to see *Swan Lake* or that one where they all dance like toy soldiers. These people are even ruder. When our theatre manager retired, they asked him what he wanted as his farewell gift — and he asked for a machine gun at the top of the stairs to gun down the ballet audience. But I think in the end he got a clock — which is a shame. But I just did the one summer and I wasn't invited back. I talked too much, striking up conversations with everybody when they didn't really want to be distracted from their grand evening out. Two minutes before the curtain rises and with a queue of one hundred people behind them, people don't really want to be asked where they live, how they got here, or whether their breasts are real. Well, I just comment on the first thing that pops into my head. In my experience, if the breasts *are* real, then they're quite flattered by the question. And their husbands beam with pride like they've just presented their new born twins. It's only when the breasts are false and pumped with gelatine that the question causes offence and a great look of astonishment that the thought even occurred to you. But honestly, it's pretty obvious they're fake when some seventy-year-old dame is standing there in front of you with upright tits that could poke your eye out. It's perfectly clear that God had no hand in those. But like I say — they didn't invite me back...

She spots a waiter with a tray of food passing nearby

Ooh — vol-au-vent!

She reaches for one but misses out as he walks right past her

Bastard. I thought we had an agreement. (*Looking across the room*) There's bound to be some nearer the drinks table...

She sips her champagne

Well — maybe I'll give it a go. It's really not that far — and lovely Bill will be waiting there to greet me. It's all to do with nerves and attitude. Just calm yourself. (*Making her voice more elegant*) If you think like a lady and talk like a lady — you'll walk like a lady. (*Slight pause*)Yes. Quite right.

She drinks the rest of the champagne in one gulp and then, after preparing herself, she staggers across the room as though walking on a sheet of ice. She makes a final lurch for the end of the room, apologizing to various people as she bumps into them on her way. She lands in a heap on a chair by the table of drinks

And if it walks like a duck and talks like a duck — it's a duck! Anyway here we are. Where's Bill...? Bill? Maybe he popped out for ice. (*To another guest*) Hallo! New heels. Nightmare. Should have worn my trainers. (*Looking at the woman's feet*) Your shoes are lovely. Where did you...? Jimmy Choo? Is that the shop or the man that bought them for you? ... Oh, right — he's the designer... "Jimmy Choo". Sounds more like a take-away... Were they expensive? ... How much!? Bloody hell — you could have yourself a new face for that. (*The woman leaves*) Oh, — you off already?

SECTION 11

Susan notices a half-empty bottle of the champagne on the table

Susan You forgot your bottle of... Oh well. Waste not, want not.

She refills her champagne glass, looking around at the other guests as she does so, and throwing out the odd wave

   (*In her elegant voice*) Oh, we're all so sophisticated. Shall we go to the ballet?

This distraction causes her to over-fill the glass and the champagne spills all over the table

   (*In her common voice*) Oh shit and bugger it! Bill! I need a cloth. Bill!

Still no sign of Bill

   Isn't there a cloth around? This is going to go everywhere.

She searches for a cloth but with no success

   Oh hell — only one thing for it...

She reached into her bra and pulls out several folds of toilet roll. She uses this to mop up the champagne. Then she casually throws the wet toilet roll into a handy ice bucket

   Well, that's one job done — but now the other problem. (*She looks down at her chest*) I'm more east than west.

She removes the toilet roll stuffed into the other side of her bra, tears it in two and stuffs the reduced portions evenly into either side. As she is in the middle of doing this, Bill returns

   Oh, Bill! (*She is embarrassed*) I was just — don't look. I'm just... No, it has to be done. Or looking at them will make you sea sick... There. How are you? ... Oh yes, I'm fine. Though my feet are killing me. I bought some heels so I looked more elegant — wanted to make an effort for you. And dress up nice. (*Slight pause*) I presume you didn't get the chance... Well, no, you're working, really, aren't you.

Half-partying, half-working. Split down the middle. Like me — half-partying, half making a complete idiot of myself. It's called multi-tasking. ... Oh, do you like it? (*Referring to her dress*) I bought it today in a shop in Sydney. It's not the perfect size — pinches a bit. But it was reasonably easy to get on and will be simple to get off — not that I'm advertizing. And I've put on heels. ... Oh, you saw me! Well — at least I made it here in one piece. And no accidents caused along the way, thank God. ... Oh, did I? Well, the vol-au-vents might as well be all over the floor, I never got any. ... Oh yes, I'm having a fantastic time. I've been everywhere this week — on boat trips and bus trips and tours of lovely buildings. And I've eaten crabs and creatures and bugs and barbecued God knows what. And I've been to the beach — every day — as you know, and I even went to Kirribilli where you've got your caravan. Didn't see it, though. ... Yes, I imagine they are a bit claustrophobic — but it's just you living there isn't it? And I'm sure your caravan's lovely inside. Small and uncomfortable but it does the job. Like a penis.

She sips her champagne and turns away from Bill for a moment

I can't believe I said that. (*She thinks of how she might recover from this and turns back to Bill*) Not that I'm an expert! (*Slight pause*) Sorry — I'm a bit nervous. I just talk... I shouldn't have come — I feel a bit out of place. I'm always the first to leave any party. Which is a shame because I love to dance and I love to have a good time. But then other people turn up and spoil everything. And *you* make me even more nervous. ... Well of couse you do — you're just standing there all gorgeous and suddenly I'm a giggling twenty year old all over again. So here I am — going around full circle. (*Slight pause*) Do you dance, Bill? No — I didn't think so. Very few men do. I mean they force themselves to bounce about a bit when essential — but ballroom dancing, or any kind of old fashioned type couples dancing — well, men that do that really are a dying breed. Fortunately — I'm perfectly used to dancing on my own. ... No, no, don't worry — it's what we unmarried old ladies do best. Could you put something nice on to play for me. A CD with a romantic song or something. ... Thank you.

Bill wanders off

He's so sweet...

She looks down at her feet

I can't dance in these shoes. There'll be no survivors.

She slips off her shoes and places them on the bar. She then finishes her glass of champagne

(*Calling off*) You can refill either the glass or the slippers, I'll leave it up to you.

At this moment, the background piano music stops and a song track begins. Jon McLaughlin singing So Close (*from the soundtrack of the film* Enchanted *or another song that has a similar feeling*). *Susan approves of the music and gives Bill a thumbs up. She then, in bare feet, makes her way to the centre of the floor. As the song plays in its entirety, Susan will dance to the music. At first she just stands and feels the music. Then she begins to gently sway. After a little while, her arms slowly wrap around her body, hugging herself. She closes her eyes. After a few moments more, she reaches her hand backwards as though searching for the hand of someone behind her (the same physical action that she did during the beach scene). She opens her eyes and we see a moment of deep regret that there is nobody there to take a hand. She takes a deep breath. Then closes her eyes again. Slowly, her hands reach out to take the hands of an imaginary man. This done, she proceeds to dance around the room as though being led by an elegant gentleman. This should be skilfully done so that we can imagine her dancing partner as clearly as she can.*

When the music swells, the dance becomes bigger, spinning around and reaching every part of the dance floor. As this happens, her eyes open and she shows great joy. She dances well, as though lost in a dream and this sequence should be tightly and carefully choreographed. As the song begins to draw to an end, the dance finishes and Susan bows to her imaginary partner. She then walks to the corner of the room where the scene began. The final notes of the song play out. She turns to us

Why is it that when I first see an attractive man, I want to run towards him? Then when he seems interested in me, I can hardly stop myself from running away. It's like a storm that suddenly catches hold of me. It's all I can do to just cling on. My heart says one thing but my brain — not known for its levels of activity — suddenly goes into hyper-drive. So many unanswerable questions... How will it turn out? Will he grow to hate me? Is love just another source of pain? Can a woman at my age really challenge her heart? Can a man and woman ever really find joy in Kirribilli? What about the cats!? (*Slight pause*) And — of course — can he really love me for who I am? That's the thing, you see. I need to change. I know that. I have to sort myself out.

There has to be a reason nobody has ever... If anybody is ever going to want me, then I have to stop being — *me*. Being crazy me. Problem is — it's the only thing I'm any good at. So desperate for love and with a personality that would send any love screaming out of the building. I'm not even sure how I ended up so eccentric. My parents weren't eccentric. I live a relatively normal life. I eat a balanced diet — meat, veg, potatoes, pudding — more pudding. And if I try and change, it won't last long. Or — at least — it won't be *real*. My friends think they've changed themselves enormously. But they haven't. It's just a veneer, a bit of extra gloss. I still see those silly twenty-year-old girls. Though, my God, they've done their best to bury them... Not me though. Still the little lost fool in the corner of the room. The one that didn't change. The one that can't.

More vol-au-vents pass within reach

Yes, I will have one of those, thank you. ... Hello?! (*She misses out again*) It's like they can't even see me! I'm the invisible blob. I'll end up starving to death. Thank God for room service. They do a cold hamburger with limp salad that's second to none. Maybe I should just go back to my room.

She looks towards Bill

Getting busy at the bar now. Bill is lost in the crowd. I should leave him to it. Let him be with his work mates. Actually, I could start packing. I fly home in less than thirty-six hours. Back to the old place. Back to the old me. Yes, better get the suitcases organized... That's the thing about being here in the corner of the room. It's always easy to make an exit.

Susan quietly exits

Black-out. Music fades up — Charles Aznavour singing Dance in the Old Fashioned Way

SCENE 6

SECTION 12

Lights rise again on the bar area. A cocktail menu stands open on the bar, with a note attached to it. Susan enters. She is wearing an Australian hat with corks hanging from it on strings. She carries two incredibly heavy

suitcases which she half drags across the floor and stashes behind the
bar hidden from our view. She also has a small shoulder bag. The music
fades out

Susan These cases are definitely heavier than when I arrived. I suppose
it's the three weeks of hotel shampoo bottles. It's a shame not to take
them, you never know when one might come in handy. I've also bought
three jars of Vegemite and this lovely hat... I'm such a sophisticated
shopper.

She removes the hat

I also purchased a boomerang for Julia because I thought it would
remind her of her boyfriends. She throws them away with great force
and then gets disappointed when they don't come back... There was no
point getting anything for Pauline because I never see her — though
next time she calls to announce a suicide I can tell her all about my
trip. I saw lots of things Debra would have liked, but of course...
Anyway here we are — packed and ready to go. Another long flight —
but I'm sure I'll find someone to chat to. I've upgraded to "premium"
economy which gives you five inches more leg room plus the stewards
smile occasionally. So won't that be a treat. You get your own area of
the cabin and they separate you by drawing a curtain across like you're
all about to be cremated. But its purpose is so that you don't have to
mix with the riff-raff in economy. I wonder what nice man I'll sit next
to? We'll have so much to chat about. Well, *I* will, at any rate. Whether
he joins in or not is completely optional. I'll just rattle on regardless.
I've noticed that there reaches a point when talking to a man where
their eyes glaze over and then at thirty second intervals they chuckle or
smile or nod in agreement even though it's completely inappropriate
to what you're talking about. I think men think that they're fooling us
into believing they're listening when we actually know perfectly well
they're adding up the football scores or wondering what you look like
naked. Or in my case trying everything in their power *not* to imagine
what I look like naked.

She sees the note attached to the bar menu

Oh, — I think that note might be for me...

She unclips the note from the menu and reads it

It's from Bill. (*She mimics his Australian voice*) "Dear Susan —

wishing you a terrific journey home — try not to distract the pilot with those legs of yours. Come back soon. We here down under miss you already. Bill." (*Back to her own voice*) And there are three kisses — that's two more than I ever got out of him. Darling man... He couldn't be here to see me off in person. It was the disco again last night and he was working till four am. So he'll be back at base, snoring away in his home on wheels. I've already written him a note back.

She takes a folded letter out of her pocket and reads it to us

First the chapter list — "Sorry, please, don't, hope, thank you, why." (*She now fills in the blanks for us*) "Dear Bill... *Sorry* for dancing on the bar and upsetting the tray of vol-au-vents. *Please* keep in touch and send me letters about all your adventures in my absence. One day I might even try email — but as I'm still struggling to operate the toaster, this might be some way off. *Don't* forget to play Earth, Wind and Fire at the disco, as you never know when some old lady will fancy a boogie. *Hope* you will find *yourself* a nice lady one day with a caravan to call her own. *Thank you* for — (*She pauses*) — for helping me realize that there's nothing wrong with growing old. The only crime is *feeling* old. You've turned me into a twenty-year-old again — give or take the dodgy hips and the uncontrollable flatulence...

She stops, looks concerned, takes out a pen and then crosses out this last sentence

Why don't you come and visit me one day. Going around the world can be quite a treat. Everyone should try it at least once every forty years. Love, Susan."

She folds up the letter

I put just two kisses as I've been told it's always best to leave them wanting more — though them wanting "more" is not my problem — it's them wanting anything at all. Although I must admit, there did seem a funny sort of chemistry between me and Bill. And I suppose there might be Bills everywhere — if you bother to look... Though it's not like *this* Bill is *that* far away. It's only the other side of the world... Maybe just two more kisses for luck.

She unfolds the letter and writes two more kisses

There. Done.

She folds the letter away again and attaches it to the menu

Goodbye, my friend.

She lays the menu down flat on the bar. In doing so, she reveals what was hidden behind the menu when it was standing — a mini birthday cake with a single candle and a lighter to its side. She is surprised and touched and puts her hands to her mouth in enchanted disbelief

Oh, Bill...! I'm speechless...

She pauses for a moment. Then she takes the lighter and lights the single candle. She watches it flicker, smiling. Then she closes her eyes and makes a wish. Then she blows out the candle

Happy birthday, Susan... It won't be long before I'll have to plan my next trip here — on my next big birthday occasion. Which will be in — well, I'm not waiting another forty years — I'll look like Tutankhamun. Sixty-one perhaps — or sixty and a half even. That's got a better ring to it. Hopefully he'll still be working here. If not, I can track him down. Although his home is mobile, of course...

She puts the cake carefully into her bag

I'll save this for the journey. Maybe the air stewards will sing me happy birthday inbetween smiles. ... Fool that I am, I haven't bought Bill anything. And I really should have done. He's not got anything to remind him of me. Unless...

She roots around in her shoulder bag and finds the two small tins of sardines she brought out with her

Ah! Sardines! There — I knew I'd find something.

She puts the tins of sardines on the bar

It's not exactly a box of chocolates, but — at least it'll be a surprise. And they do come from back home... And oh how strange it will be going home. Walking down the street and seeing the same old faces, people whose lives have just carried on exactly the same, while mine was spinning into something completely surprising. The old ladies who live nearby walk around the town as though they are carrying a couple of unbelievably heavy suitcases — even though their hands are empty. Bent over, strained, the pressures of the world weighing them down. I've got my own baggage too. But it ever so suddenly feels as light as air.

Susan goes behind the bar to collect her suitcases. Unseen by the audience, the cases are swapped over so that she now actually carries two identical empty ones. However she mimes that they are still the original heavy cases. She struggles into the middle of the floor. As she approaches, the music Boogie Wonderland *begins to fade in. She stops in her tracks. Then she begins to move her shoulders and bottom to the rhythm of the music. After a few moments, it rises to full volume and Susan begins to dance joyfully. She raises the two suitcases into the air and spins around in circles with the luggage flying around her, light as air*

The Lights fade to blackout

The music starts to fade out, to be replaced by an airport announcement during which the scene changes to a Sydney airport lounge

FINAL SECTION

All of the actresses who have played Susan now gather on stage, each with suitcases. The dialogue in this next section is shared between the actresses. How the dialogue is divided up is up to the director

Australian airport announcement: "Passengers are reminded that they may not take any liquids or sharp objects in their hand luggage. However, perfumes and bottled water are available after the security area at over-inflated prices. Please keep all your belongings with you, as suspicious items and suspicious people may be taken away and destroyed

Lights rise on Susan at the airport. She turns to face us, still holding her cases

Susan At the end of the day — there was a choice. Stay in Sydney, do my best to change, try things out with Bill. Or — go home, be the same person, wave goodbye to Bill. I'd decided on option two. I'd be alone — but at least I'd be myself. I was at peace with that. But then came that little birthday cake.

She puts down the cases

I mean — who'd have ever thought — that he'd have ever thought — of something like that. It was the smallest birthday cake I've ever had. And the grandest. So I bought him this.

She takes a ring box out of her pocket and opens it to show us the simple gold band inside

No, no — It's not an engagement ring — I mean — (*A little loudly*) I'm not crazy!

Somebody passes by at this point

Sorry — didn't mean to frighten you — just talking to myself. Where are you off to? Brazil!? Oh be careful — there's a fish there that swims up your penis. Keep your legs crossed. (*She waves*) Bye then. (*Back to the ring*) Now where was I? Oh yes — "crazy". This is a *friendship* ring. It says that I want to keep in touch. It says I like him very much. It says — I'm coming back. Oh yes — didn't I tell you? Booked it this morning. I've another flight here in about three months. Well, ninety-two days and fourteen hours to be precise. I thought it would be impossible because of leaving my three pedigree cats behind, not to mention the huge cost. And then I came up with a solution — *sell* the cats...! I'm so clever sometimes I have to pinch myself. Bill is coming to meet me here just before I board the flight. That's when I'll give him this. I hope he likes it. It's not real gold. But it's the thought that counts. And giving him this — and telling him how much he means to me — will be the last thing I do on this adventure. And the *first* thing I do on a *new* adventure.

She puts the ring away

How *that* story ends, I can't tell you. But I can tell you how this one ends — flying home.

She picks up the cases

So off we go then...

All the actresses now exit together apart from one of them, who delivers on her own the final moments of the play

Susan walks a few steps towards the exit, but bumps into her fellow passenger from the outbound flight

Oh, hallo again! It's James, isn't it! We sat next to each other on the way out. Remember? (*Repeating what he says*) "You won't forget it for the rest of your life" — well, that's very flattering, I must say! You won't believe this — but you wrote your number down wrong. Bet you feel a fool... We must be on the same flight home — what row are you in? ... Same as me! We can carry on talking from where we left off! ... Are you all right? You've gone white as a sheet. You should take something — you don't want to be chucking up all over the plane. ... Bye, then.

She watches him head off, then turns to face us

See you soon...

Susan smiles at us. We hear a final blast of Sinatra singing the last bars of the song Come Fly With Me. *Susan walks to the exit with her cases as the Lights fade. We reach black-out as the song ends*

THE END

FURNITURE AND PROPERTY LIST

SCENE 1

On stage: A row of plastic seats. A coffee vending machine

Off stage: Large plastic tray. *In it:* jacket, jewellery, purse,
watch, tickets, passport, a bag containing a complete
toilet roll, 2 tins of sardines
A pair of shoes, a belt, coins, a folded
newspaper article (**Susan**)
Cup of vending machine coffee (**Stage Manager**)

SCENE 2

Strike: A row of plastic seats. A coffee vending machine

Set: Bar with a hook on it, bar stool

On stage: 4 cocktails, empty champagne glasses

Off stage: Wrist-watch, handbag. *In it:* ear-plugs. (**Susan**)

SCENE 3

Strike: Bar with a hook on it, bar stool

Set: Garden seat

Off stage: Ear plugs, handbag. *In it:* small bag of aeroplane
nuts. (**Susan**)

SCENE 4

Strike: Garden seat

Set: Parasol

Off stage: Towel. lunch box *In it:* a doughnut, ham sandwiches,
a carton of apple juice with a straw (**Susan**)

Personal: Sunglasses (**Susan**)

Scene 5

Strike: Parasol

Set: Bar, table of drinks (including a half-empty bottle of
               champagne and an ice bucket), a chair

Off stage: Champagne flute, some money, folds of toilet roll
               "bra-padding" (**Susan**)

Scene 6

Set: Cocktail menu (with note attached), a mini
               birthday cake with a single candle, lighter,
               2 empty suitcases

Off stage: Australian hat with corks, 2 heavy suitcases,
               small shoulder bag. *In it:* 2 tins of sardines, pen
               A folded letter (**Susan**)

Final Section

Strike: Bar, cocktail menu, 2 suitcases

Off stage: 2 empty suitcases, ringbox with gold ring (**Susan**)

LIGHTING PLOT

Practical fitting required: Glitter-ball
Various interior and exterior settings

SCENE 1

To open: Airport interior lighting

Cue 1	**Susan** exits *Snap black-out*	(Page 11)

SCENE 2

To open: Bar lights rise

Cue 2	**Susan**: "... and he was a goner." *Lights dim*	(Page 16)
Cue 3	**Susan**: "Whether it's completely empty or not." *Glitter-ball effect starts*	(Page 16)
Cue 4	**Susan** walks around the outside of the stage *Lights transform into a moonlit hotel garden*	(Page 19)

SCENE 3

To open: Moonlit hotel garden

Cue 5	**Susan** wanders unsteadily across the stage *Lights fade to black-out*	(Page 22)

SCENE 4

To open: Daytime beach lighting

Cue 6	**Susan**: "I can't wait to see the look of surprise on her face…!" *Snap black-out*	(Page 27)

SCENE 5

To open: Hotel cocktail party lighting

Cue 7	**Susan** exits	(Page 34)
	Black-out	

SCENE 6

To open: Bar lights rise

Cue 8	**Susan** dances with her suitcases	(Page 38)
	Lights fade to black-out	

FINAL SECTION

Cue 9	End of airport announcement	(Page 38)
	Lights rise	
Cue 10	Music: Frank Sinatra singing *"Come Fly With Me"*	(Page 40)
	Lights fade to black-out as the song ends	

EFFECTS PLOT

Cue 1   Opening of SCENE 1   (Page 1)
         Music: Frank Sinatra singing "Come Fly With Me"

Cue 2   **Susan**: "...or buys some useless magazines."   (Page 5)
         Airport announcement: "Flight one-seven-four to Paris,
         please board at gate twelve. Last call for flight two-two-nine
         to Buenos Aires — board at gate twenty-seven"

Cue 3   **Susan** puts coins in the vending machine   (Page 6)
         Airport announcement: "We remind passengers that for
         security reasons, they should keep their belongings with
         them at all times. Any item found left on its own will be
         taken away by the airport police and immediately
         destroyed. In accordance with the government's
         announcement of a red danger level for possible imminent
         attack, passengers should report any suspicious persons
         or actions to a security officer. Armed law enforcement
         operates in this airport. Always be vigilant and aware
         of potential terrorism... Have a relaxed and pleasant flight."

Cue 4   **Susan**: "But it isn't — believe me."   (Page 10)
         Airport announcement: "Announcing the boarding
         of flight QS one-seven-two to Sydney Australia."

Cue 5   **Susan**: "That's me!"   (Page 10)
         Airport announcement: "Now boarding at gate
         seventeen."

Cue 6   **Susan** drops all her bags on the floor   (Page 11)
         Airport announcement: "Final announcement for Flight
         QS one-seven-two to Sydney Australia. All passengers
         immediately to gate thirty-five please... And that includes
         you, Susan. So get off your fat arse and get on the bleedin'
         plane."

Cue 7   **Susan**: "...down to be more precise."   (Page 11)
         Airport announcement: ""Susan! Are we going to have
         to drag you on to this bloody plane?"

Cue 8   Opening of SCENE 2   (Page 11)
             Music: Frank Sinatra singing "Come Fly With Me"

Cue 9   Opening of SECTION 6   (Page 17)
             Stereo music: "Boogie Wonderland" by Earth Wind & Fire,
             followed by something "violently contemporary"

Cue 10   **Susan** puts in left then right earplugs   (Page 17)
             Music stops from the left and then from the right

Cue 11   **Susan** wanders unsteadily across the stage   (Page 22)
             Mmusic rises: Men At Work singing "I Come
             From a Land Down Under"

Cue 12   Opening of SCENE 4   (Page 22)
             Music fades

Cue 13   *Black-out*   (Page 27)
             Piano music

Cue 14   Opening of SCENE 5   (Page 27)
             Piano music fades to background level

Cue 15   **Susan** "...I'll leave it up to you."   (Page 33)
             Piano music stops, music: Jon McLaughlin
             singing "So Close" starts

Cue 16   **Susan** *exits. Black-out*   (Page 34)
             Music: Charles Aznavour singing "Dance in the
             Old Fashioned Way" starts

Cue 17   Opening of SCENE 6   (Page 35)
             Music fades out

Cue 18   **Susan** *collects her suitcases from behind the bar* (Page 38)
             Music: "Boogie Wonderland"fades in the rises
             to full volume

Cue 19   Lights fade to black-out   (Page 38)
             Music fades

Cue 20   Opening of FINAL SECTION   (Page 38)
             Airport announcement: "Passengers are reminded
             that they may not take any liquids or sharp objects in
             their hand luggage. However, perfumes and bottled
             water are available after the security area at over-
             inflated prices. Please keep all your belongings

with you, as suspicious items and suspicious
people may be taken away and destroyed.

Cue 21   **Susan** "Bye then."   (Page 40)
            Music: Last bars of Frank Sinatra singing
            "Come Fly With Me"

Lightning Source UK Ltd.
Milton Keynes UK
UKOW05f1237290117
293104UK00014B/198/P